IT'LL NEVER WORK

PLANES

AND HELICOPTERS

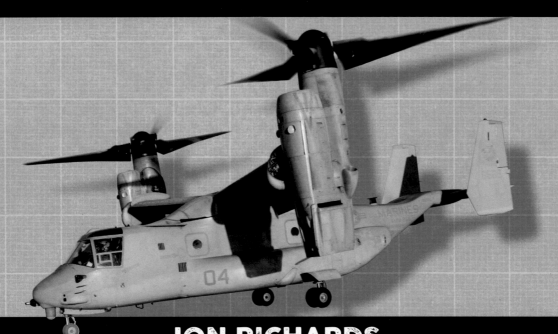

JON RICHARDS

W

FRANKLIN WATTS

LONDON • SYDNEY

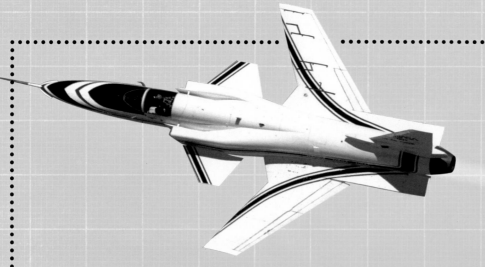

Franklin Watts
First published in Great Britain in 2016 by
The Watts Publishing Group

Copyright © The Watts Publishing
Group, 2016

Credits
Conceived, designed and edited by
Tall Tree Ltd
Series Editor: David John
Series Designer: Jonathan Vipond

ISBN 978 1 4451 5025 3

Printed in China

Franklin Watts
An imprint of
Hachette Children's Group
Part of The Watts Publishing Group
Carmelite House
50 Victoria Embankment
London EC4Y 0DZ

An Hachette UK Company
www.hachette.co.uk

www.franklinwatts.co.uk

Picture credits:
t-top, b-bottom, l-left, r-right,
c-centre, m-middle
All images public domain unless
otherwise indicated:
Front cover mcr, 1, 19cr courtesy of US Navy, front
cover cr, 2, 27c courtesy of NASA, front cover bl, 15cl
istockphoto.com/EdStock, front cover blc, 23c
dreamstime.com/Nfx702, back cover tr, 17l dreamstime.
com/Paul Martin, 3br, 23t dreamstime.com/
Stephenmeese, 4b dreamstime.com/Rinus Baak, 5bl all
istockphoto.com/ZU_09, 6bl dreamstime.com/Isselee,
6bc dreamstime.com/Vasyl Helevachuk, 6br
dreamstime.com/Igor Usatyuk, 13t all dreamstime.
com/Miro9966, 14l dreamstime.com/I4lcocl2, 15t
courtesy of NASA, 16l courtesy of NASA, 17tr
dreamstime.com/Andrew Oxley, 18b Getty Images/
Central Press, 19br courtesy of US Navy, 22
dreamstime.com/Igor Dolgov, 26bl, 27t, 29
courtesy of NASA.

CONTENTS

TAKING TO THE SKIES

For thousands of years, humans have gazed at birds, wondering how they can take off and fly through the air. Would human flight ever be possible, or was it just pie in the sky?

👉 MASTERS OF THE AIR

Birds use their wings to fly, either by flapping them or using them to catch air currents to keep them aloft. Their wings are covered with special flight feathers. These give the wings their distinctive shape so that the bird can fly in a particular way, whether this is soaring like an eagle or hovering like a hummingbird.

A hummingbird can flap its wings up and down as well as back and forth up to 80 times per second. This allows it to hover next to a flower and feed off the flower's nectar.

ICARUS

According to Greek myth, Icarus and his father Daedalus were locked in a tower. They tried to flee by making wings from feathers stuck together with wax. While his father managed to fly to freedom, Icarus flew too close to the Sun. The heat from the Sun melted the wax in his wings and he fell to his death.

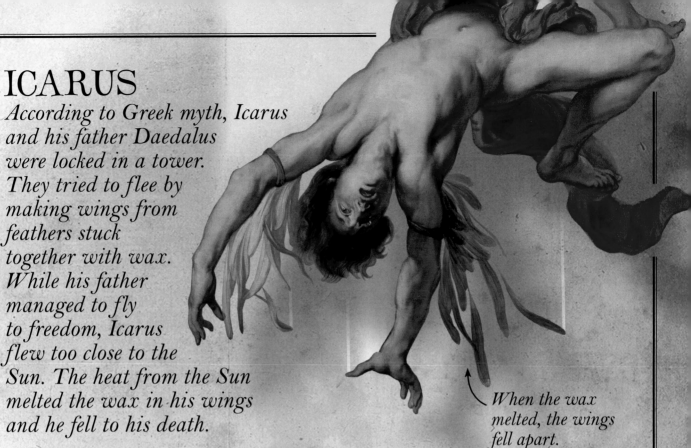

When the wax melted, the wings fell apart.

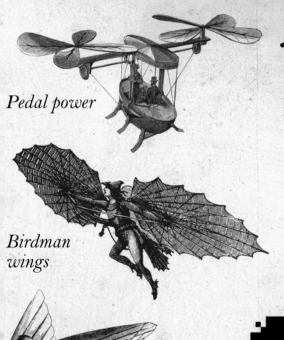

Pedal power

Birdman wings

Flapping wings operated by feet

☞ TRYING TO GET OFF THE GROUND

Other crazy flying ideas have included strapping large bird-like canvas wings to a person's arms, and propellers turned by bicycle pedals. None of these inventions ever made it into the air. So how was powered, controlled flight ever going to achieve takeoff?

MODERN FLIGHT

Today, we take flying for granted. At any one time, there are about 5,000 planes in the sky over the USA alone. Worldwide, more than 102,000 passenger flights take off every day.

EARLY FLIGHT

While the first flying machines used a lot of hot air, the first real planes and gliders had to wait until someone developed the right wing shape.

UP, UP AND AWAY ... 👉

One of the first successful flights was made in a hot-air balloon. Many people believed that living things would die above a certain height. In September 1783 at Versailles near Paris, the Montgolfier brothers set out to prove them wrong. They put a sheep, a duck and a cockerel into a basket beneath a balloon and sent it high into the sky using hot air from a fire beneath to lift the balloon into the air. The flight lasted eight minutes and the animals were unharmed. Two months later, the brothers built a bigger balloon and made the first piloted flight with people on board.

The Montgolfier balloon was decorated with the face of the French king, Louis XVI.

6

TOUGH JUSTICE

In the year CE599, Emperor Wenxuan from Northern Qi, China, amused himself by watching prisoners being forced to throw themselves from a tower while strapped to a kite. All died, except for one, Yuan Huangtou, who managed to glide over the city walls. His reward for this daring feat? He was executed for the crimes he had committed!

HOW DO WINGS WORK?

So just how do wings keep things off the ground? The secret lies in their shape, which is called an aerofoil. It has a curved upper surface and a flat lower surface, which causes air flowing over the wing to travel faster than air flowing under the wing. The faster-moving air above the wing has lower pressure than the slower-moving air below and this pushes the wing up.

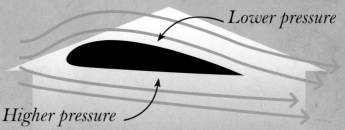

Lower pressure

Higher pressure

But this isn't the whole story. A plane's wing is tilted backwards slightly, which is known as the angle of attack. This directs air down, which pushes the wing up, creating lift.

GLIDER KING 👉

In the 1880s, German engineer Otto Lilienthal made many flights using simple hang gliders. He proved that lift could be produced through the curve of the wing, rather than through 'flapping flight'.

POWERED FLIGHT

Using hot air and gliding on wings will only get you so far. To stay in the air for long periods of time you need something to power you through the sky.

👉 STEAM POWER

Early ideas for powered flight included having pilots pedalling frantically, or even strapping a flock of birds to an aircraft. More serious plans involved the use of steam engines, but early versions of these were too heavy. However, French inventor Félix du Temple de la Croix built his own lightweight steam engine and fixed it to a plane. After several failed attempts to generate enough power, du Temple succeeded in performing a short manned flight in 1874, which may have been the first powered flight in history, nearly thirty years before the Wright brothers' famous attempt.

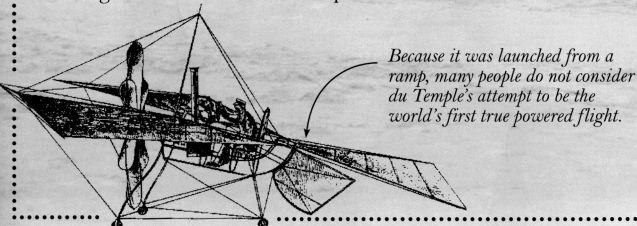

Because it was launched from a ramp, many people do not consider du Temple's attempt to be the world's first true powered flight.

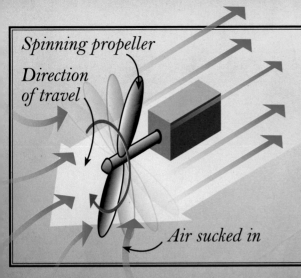

Spinning propeller

Direction of travel

Air sucked in

PROPELLER POWER

The first powered aircraft used propellers driven by engines to push them through the air. A propeller acts like a spinning wing. As it spins around, it pushes air behind it, which, in turn, pushes the aircraft forwards.

Orville Wright's first flight at Kitty Hawk, in North Carolina, USA, lasted only 12 seconds and covered just 37 metres.

WRIGHT BROTHERS

On 17 December 1903, Orville Wright performed the first powered, controlled flight in a biplane he had built with his brother Wilbur. This was the result of years of trial and error, in which the brothers had tested various gliders using data from the research of German aviator Otto Lilienthal, whose death in a glider crash in 1896 inspired them to continue his work. The biplane was fitted with a custom-built lightweight engine that powered two wooden propellers.

PLANES AT WAR

Less than fifteen years after the Wright brothers' first flight, aircraft were being used during the First World War (1914–1918) These ranged from small, fast fighter planes designed to attack other planes, to large bombers built to drop explosives on enemy troops.

PASSENGER FLIGHT

When the First World War ended in 1918, thousands of war planes were left unused – until some bright spark had the idea of using them to fly people around the globe.

CURTISS JN4 'JENNY'

Although it was designed in the USA as a military training aircraft, the 'Jenny' saw action after the war in many civilian roles. These included carrying individual paying passengers, transporting mail and even performing acrobatic stunts at air shows.

Passenger and pilot sat exposed to the elements in open cockpits.

75

FLYING TOILET

When it first flew in 1919, the Handley Page Type W became the first airliner designed with an on-board toilet – what did passengers do before that?

A380

Trimotor

UNDER PRESSURE

People have long known from climbing mountains that thin air at high altitude can cause sickness and death. So when US pilot John Macready set an altitude record of 11,000 metres in 1921, he took an oxygen supply with him. He survived the flight, but he was unprepared for the low air pressure, which caused his heart to enlarge! The solution was to keep the air inside a cabin at high pressure. The first airliner with a pressurised cabin was the 1958 Boeing 307 Stratoliner.

Boeing 307 Stratoliner

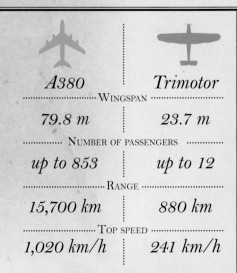

A Boeing Stratoliner could carry passengers in comfort at altitudes of more than 6,000 metres.

LITTLE AND LARGE

Today's super jumbos can carry nearly 850 passengers and crew over thousands of kilometres. The largest modern airliner is the Airbus A380, which has two decks (one on top of the other) and a wingspan that's almost as big as a football pitch – far bigger than a popular airliner from the 1920s, the Ford Trimotor.

A380	Trimotor
WINGSPAN	
79.8 m	23.7 m
NUMBER OF PASSENGERS	
up to 853	up to 12
RANGE	
15,700 km	880 km
TOP SPEED	
1,020 km/h	241 km/h

THE JET ENGINE

While propeller engines are strong enough to get aircraft off the ground, they have limits. To go REALLY fast, you need an engine that pushes a plane along by blowing gases out of the back, such as a jet.

JET POWER

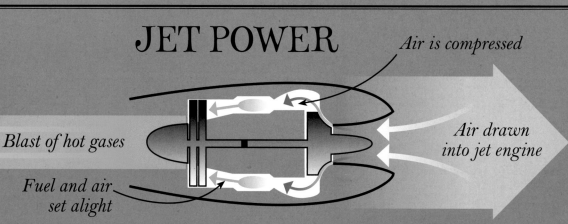

Air is compressed

Air drawn into jet engine

Blast of hot gases

Fuel and air set alight

Jet engines work by drawing in large volumes of air, compressing (squeezing) it, mixing it with petroleum fuel and then setting light to it. This produces a blast of hot gases, which roar out of the back of the engine, pushing it forwards.

ANCIENT ENGINE

Jet engines are far from a new idea. In the first century BCE, Greek inventors built a device called an aeolipile – a spinning ball powered by jets of steam. However, it would be 2,000 years before inventors built a jet engine that could fly an aircraft.

The German Messerschmitt Me 262 was the first jet fighter to see action in the Second World War.

DAWN OF THE JET

In the 1930s, two engineers, Frank Whittle in the UK and Hans von Ohain in Germany, both designed and built jet engines for military aircraft. First off the ground was a Heinkel He 178 in 1939, powered by an engine built by von Ohain. Both the UK and Germany had jets in active service towards the end of the Second World War (1939–1945).

PASSENGER JETS

After the war, jet engines were fitted to civilian jet liners. The de Haviland Comet became the world's first commercial jet liner in 1952. However, a flaw in the Comet's design (it had square rather than round windows) caused stresses in the plane's metal fuselage. Three of them broke up in mid-flight and crashed. From 1958, the Comet was widely replaced by the more reliable Boeing 707.

de Haviland Comet

FASTER THAN SOUND

One of the biggest hurdles in high-speed flight is breaking the sound barrier by flying faster than the speed of sound. At these speeds, high pressures and extreme conditions can tear an aircraft apart!

Supermarine Spitfire

👉 EARLY CLAIMS

During the Second World War, several pilots claimed to have broken the sound barrier, in planes as diverse as the British propeller-driven Supermarine Spitfire, the jet-powered Messerschmitt Me 262 and the Messerschmitt Me 163, which was powered by a rocket instead of a jet. However, none of these claims could be proven and many suspect that they were caused by incorrect instrument readings.

THE SPEED OF SOUND

The speed of sound is measured using Mach numbers, where Mach 1 is the speed of sound and Mach 2 is twice the speed of sound. How fast sound travels depends on the temperature and humidity of the air and how high up you are. At sea level, Mach 1 is about 1,225 kilometres per hour, but at an altitude of about 35,000 metres it is about 720 kilometres per hour.

BREAKING THE BARRIER

The first aircraft proven to break the sound barrier was a US Bell X-1 rocket plane on 14 October 1947. The Bell X-1's key innovations included a cone-shaped nose, and thin, sharp wings, as it had been discovered that rounded edges could not be kept stable at supersonic speeds. The tail had a powered stabiliser that controlled the aircraft under intense aerodynamic forces.

The Bell X-1 reached a speed of 1,100 km/h, or Mach 1.06.

6062

CONCORDE V CONCORDSKI

In 1976, Concorde became the first supersonic passenger airliner. Its slim shape and powerful engines gave it a speed of Mach 2, twice the speed of sound, which meant that it could cross the Atlantic Ocean in under three hours. In the Soviet Union, the Tupolev Tu-144 could also fly at Mach 2, but a rushed design led to two crashes, and the aircraft were withdrawn. After a crash in 2000, all of the Concorde aircraft were also withdrawn from service in 2003.

The Tupolev Tu-144 was also known as 'Concordski' because it looked very similar to Concorde (above).

MOVING WINGS

Birds, insects and bats move their wings to fly, don't they? So why not aircraft? These planes were built to show how moving wings could allow a plane to fly both slowly and swiftly.

The Bell X-5 could sweep its wings back at an angle of between 20° and 60° to the fuselage.

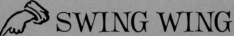

SWING WING

An early experiment with moving wings was the US Bell X-5 aircraft, built in 1951. A poorly positioned tail, however, meant that in some wing positions the planes could go into a spin, and one crashed after the pilot lost control. Despite this, the X planes showed that moving wings were effective for planes that needed to fly at a range of speeds.

Swept back 60° for fast flight

90° for normal flight

VARIABLE SWEEP WINGS

Wings that can be swept backwards and forwards are called variable sweep wings. They effectively change a plane's shape. Typically, wings that stick out straight from the fuselage are better for slow flight, while wings that are swept back are better for fast flight.

The Panavia Tornado's wings re swept out for ow-level, slow light ...

... and swept back for high-speed flight at up to 2,400 kilometres per hour, or Mach 2.2.

👉 MULTI-ROLE AIRCRAFT

The Panavia Tornado is a military aircraft designed to perform a number of roles, including low-level bombing and the high-speed pursuit of enemy aircraft. In order to perform well at both low and high speeds, the aircraft's designers have used variable sweep wings. Since it was introduced in 1974, the aircraft has seen action with the air forces of Germany, Italy, the UK and Saudi Arabia.

VERTICAL TAKEOFF

Most planes need long runways for taking off and landing. But the aircraft shown here can rise and land vertically by moving the thrust from their engines. This means that they don't need costly runways to take off and land.

FLYING BEDSTEAD

The Thrust Measuring Rig, or 'Flying Bedstead' as it was called, was a 1950s UK test aircraft invented to study vertical takeoff and landing. It may look bizarre, but it led directly to the development of military jump jets.

The 'Flying Bedstead' had several jet nozzles to lift the aircraft into the air and to control its flight.

HARRIER JUMP JET

Perhaps the most successful vertical takeoff aircraft is the Harrier Jump Jet, a fighter plane originally built in the UK by the Hawker Siddeley company. It uses movable nozzles on either side to direct thrust from the engine either straight back for normal flight or straight down to land and take off vertically or even hover in the air. It first flew in 1967 and is still in service.

Jet nozzle pointed downwards so that the Harrier can hover in the air.

19

HELICOPTER, PLANE, OR BOTH?

The V-22 Osprey is a radically different kind of military aircraft. On the ground, it looks like a strange helicopter, with its two huge rotors pointing straight up so that it can take off vertically. Once in the air, these rotors then tilt forwards so that they act like propellers, pulling the Osprey forwards at speeds of more than 500 kilometres per hour.

Osprey taking off

Rotors angled upwards

Rotors angled forwards

Osprey in flight

THE HELICOPTER

Helicopters use large, fast-spinning rotors to lift them into the air and move them through the air. They can take off and land vertically, hover and even fly backwards.

EARLY IDEAS

The idea of using rotating blades to lift things into the air dates back more than 1,500 years to early Chinese bamboo toys that featured spinning blades. In the late 15th century, Italian artist and engineer Leonardo da Vinci drew what he called an aerial screw, which featured a screw-shaped canopy of reed and linen cranked around by a man-powered shaft.

With enough rotation, the craft was meant to 'screw' through the air.

Da Vinci's machine would have been much too heavy to fly. It needed four men to rotate the central shaft.

EARLY IDEAS

The word 'helicopter' comes from the Greek words 'helix' meaning 'whirl' and 'pteron' meaning 'wing'. The word was first used in 1861 by French inventor Gustave de Ponton d'Amécourt. However, he was better at inventing words than inventing machines, as his helicopter models failed to get off the ground.

Igor Sikorsky takes off in a Sikorsky R-4 helicopter in 1946.

FIRST SUCCESSES

In 1907, French inventor Paul Cornu built a helicopter with two huge rotors. It was highly unstable and reached an altitude of just 30 centimetres! Nearly forty years later, Russian-born engineer Igor Sikorsky designed the world's first practical single-lifting-rotor helicopter. To counteract the effect of torque produced by the rotor (see below), he opted for a small rotor mounted on the tail – the model for most helicopters ever since.

IN A SPIN

As a helicopter's rotor spins in one direction, it pushes the helicopter's body in the other, a force called torque. Torque is a big problem for helicopters. Left unchecked, it would cause a helicopter to spin out of control. To overcome this, helicopters use two rotors spinning in opposite directions, or a small rotor on the helicopter's tail. This counters the effect of torque.

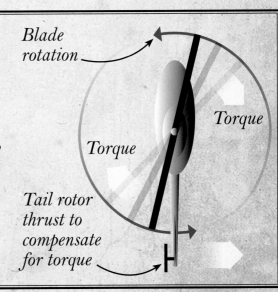

Blade rotation

Torque

Torque

Tail rotor thrust to compensate for torque

BIGGER, FASTER ... SMALLER

Because they can fly and land in places where planes cannot go, helicopters have many different roles – from fast attack aircraft to speedy people carriers and ambulances.

THE BIGGEST 👉

The Russian Mi-26 entered service in 1977 and is the world's largest helicopter. Its rotor measures 32 metres across and it is powerful enough to lift 20 tonnes of cargo – the weight of four elephants!

The single rotor has eight blades to provide enough lift for this huge helicopter.

The Westland Lynx is used as an attack and reconnaissance (observation) aircraft.

👆 THE FASTEST

The record for the world's fastest helicopter belongs to the British-built Westland Lynx. In 1986, it reached a record speed of just over 400 kilometres per hour.

👆 EVEN FASTER

The French Eurocopter X3 is an experimental aircraft known as a compound helicopter. It combines a helicopter rotor for vertical landing and takeoff with two propeller engines for high speed. At a demonstration in 2013, the X3 reached speeds of 472 kilometres per hour.

The Eurocopter's twin rotors provide fast propulsion.

23

HELICOPTER FOR ONE

In the 1950s and '60s, the US military designed a small, folding helicopter that could be dropped behind enemy lines and used by stranded pilots to escape. One of these was the Hiller YROE, which weighed just 132 kilograms and could be folded up and carried on a sled. However, it was very vulnerable to enemy fire and had no navigational instruments. As a result, the YROE never entered service.

The Hiller YROE carried one pilot.

FLYING FEATS

As if getting into the air wasn't hard enough, these pilots have all tried to push the achievements of aviation to new limits – sometimes with mixed results.

Blériot funded his aviation project with the money he'd made from designing truck headlamps.

👉 CROSS-CHANNEL FLIER

French inventor and aviator Louis Blériot designed and built many experimental aircraft at the start of the 20th century, including the world's first successful powered monoplane (plane with one wing). In July 1909, flying his own Type XI monoplane, Blériot became the first person to fly across the English Channel between France and England, winning a £1,000 prize for doing so.

Blériot takes off from Calais, France, in July 1909.

ACROSS THE ATLANTIC 👉

Flying a First World War Vickers bomber, British aviators James Alcock and Arthur Brown became the first people to fly across the Atlantic without stopping. In June 1919, they flew from Canada to Ireland in 16 hours, taking with them a supply of beer and two kittens for company.

In Ireland, Alcock and Brown mistook a bog for a landing field.

SOLO FLIGHT 👈

In 1919, a prize of $25,000 was offered to the first pilot to fly non-stop from New York to Paris. It was a US mail pilot called Charles Lindbergh who succeeded. Unlike previous pilots, Lindbergh kept his plane light. He covered the distance in 33 hours, dodging thunderclouds and flying blind through fog.

Lindbergh's main challenge was managing the weight and bulk of the fuel, which filled most of the plane.

25

AROUND THE WORLD

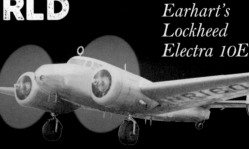

Earhart's Lockheed Electra 10E

Amelia Earhart set many flying records during her career. These included being the first woman to fly solo across the Atlantic and the first person to fly solo from Hawaii to California, USA, as well as many speed and distance records. However, during an attempt to fly around the world in 1937, she disappeared over the Pacific Ocean. To this day, mystery surrounds what happened to her.

Earhart in 1935

WEIRD AND WACKY AIRCRAFT

Manufacturers and inventors have always competed to build better and faster aircraft. Not all of their ideas have caught on ...

MANY WINGS 👉

The 1921 Ca.60 Transaereo was a flying boat built by Italian aviator Gianni Caproni, who hoped it would become a transatlantic airliner. It had nine wings, and eight engines. However, it was too tail-heavy and crashed into Lake Maggiore on a test flight.

Caproni's aircraft was designed to carry 100 passengers.

The Vought V-173 was nicknamed the 'Flying Pancake'.

👉 FLYING SAUCERS

The Vought V-173, a disc-shaped experimental aircraft built for the US Navy in 1942, demonstrated that near-vertical takeoff was possible. However, it also caused a number of reported UFO sightings by scared civilians.

The wing on the AD-1 could change angle in mid-flight.

WONKY WINGS

Something looks wrong with this aircraft, the NASA AD-1, but it could actually fly! The wing rotated so that it was at an angle of 60 degrees to the fuselage. This was to test 'oblique wing' theory, which was thought to allow the aircraft to perform better at speed.

Backwards wings for manoeuvrability

BACKWARDS WINGS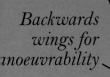

The X-29, built in 1984 by the Grumman Aerospace Corporation in the US, was designed to be unstable. Instability made this aircraft very manoeuvrable but tricky to fly – it needed six computers to make continuous adjustments to keep it in the air.

FLYING GIANTS

This whale-like aircraft was designed to swallow a whole load of cargo. The Airbus A300-600ST, or Beluga, was first built in Europe in 1994 and still flies today. It carries extra-large pieces of cargo, such as pieces of aircraft for plane manufacturer Airbus.

PEDALS AND SUNSHINE

One of the heaviest things an aircraft has to lift into the air is its fuel – but what if you could do without fuel altogether? These aircraft have tried just that, using people-power and light from the Sun as sources of energy.

PEDAL POWER 👉

On 12 June 1979, US hang-glider pilot Bryan Allen became the first person to make a human-powered flight across the English Channel, pedalling the MacCready Gossamer Albatross. The aircraft had a body and wings made from carbon fibre and polystyrene. These were covered with thin, see-through plastic, making the craft weigh just 32 kilograms!

Allen completed the crossing in 2 hours and 50 minutes, flying just 1.5 metres above the water.

SUN POWER

After the success of the Gossamer Albatross, the MacCready company built the Gossamer Penguin in 1979. This had a small electric motor that was powered by a solar panel on top of the aircraft. The designer's 13-year-old son was the test pilot as he weighed just 36 kilograms.

Cyclists follow the Penguin during a test flight in 1979.

HIGH FLIER

NASA has built a series of experimental aircraft designed to fly at very high altitudes and stay in the air for long periods of time. Solar panels covering the upper wings provide power to the propeller engines. In 2001, one of these aircraft, *Helios*, set the record for the highest sustained horizontal flight by a winged aircraft at an altitude of 29,524 metres.

Helios was powered by 14 small propeller engines.

29

AROUND THE WORLD

Solar Impulse, *designed by Swiss aeronauts André Borschberg and Bertrand Piccard, is designed to be the first solar-powered manned aircraft to fly around the world. The flight is broken into stages. The longest leg, from Japan to Hawaii, broke the record for the longest solo flight, at 117 hours, 52 minutes.*

The flight began in 2015 and will take two years to complete.

GLOSSARY

AERODYNAMIC
Relating to how gases behave and forces act on an object as it passes through the air.

AIRLINER
A large aircraft that is used to carry passengers.

ALTITUDE
The height something is above sea level.

ANGLE OF ATTACK
The angle between the oncoming air and a plane's wing. This angle pushes air downwards and this in turn pushes up on a wing and the aircraft, producing a force called lift.

AEROFOIL
The special shape of a wing that produces lower pressure above the wing than below as it moves forwards. This pressure difference pushes upwards, producing a force called lift.

BIPLANE
A plane that has two sets of wings, usually set one above the other.

CARBON FIBRE
A special material that is made up of thin strands of carbon that have been bonded together. This produces a strong but lightweight material.

FUSELAGE
The main body of an aircraft that holds the pilots, crew and any passengers and cargo.

HIGH PRESSURE
Atmospheric pressure that is greater than normal.

LIFT
The force needed to raise an object into the air. This force is produced by air passing over an aircraft's wings and is caused by the wings' special shape as well as their angle of attack.

LOW PRESSURE
Atmospheric pressure that is less than normal.

MACH
A number used to measure the speed of sound, which can vary depending on temperature and altitude. For example, the speed

30

of sound at sea level is about 340 metres per second. The speed of sound is known as Mach 1, while Mach 2 is twice the speed of sound, and so on.

NOZZLE
The exit to a jet engine or a rocket. It is used to control the direction of the blast of hot gases as they leave the engine.

PRESSURISED
The term used to describe an object whose interior air is at a higher pressure than the air around it. For example, high-flying passenger jets have a pressurised cabin, which is at a higher pressure than the air outside.

PROPELLER
A bladed wheel that spins around to push air or water backwards. This produces thrust to push the vehicle forwards.

RECONNAISSANCE
To explore or study a region and gain information about it, such as the type of terrain or the location of enemy forces.

ROTOR
The name given to the large spinning blades on a helicopter. These spin around to produce the lift needed to raise the helicopter and to push it through the air.

STABILISERS
Parts of a plane which help to control the aircraft. They are usually found at the back and are made up of a vertical stabiliser, or fin, and horizontal stabilisers, known as the tailplane.

SUPERSONIC
Travelling faster than the speed of sound. Travelling slower than the speed of sound is subsonic.

THRUST
The force that pushes a vehicle forwards.

TORQUE
A force that causes rotation.

INDEX